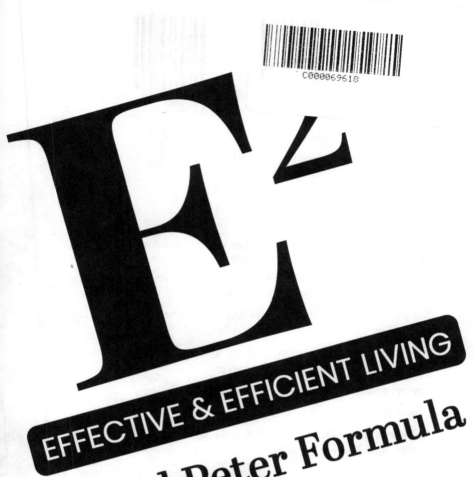

E²

EFFECTIVE & EFFICIENT LIVING

A 2nd Peter Formula

RONDA H. BAILEY

Trilogy Christian Publishers

A Wholly Owned Subsidary of Trinity Broadcasting Network

2442 Michelle Drive

Tustin, CA 92780

For information, address Trilogy Christian Publishing

Rights Department, 2442 Michelle Drive, Tustin, Ca 92780.

Trilogy Christian Publishing/ TBN and colophon are trademarks of Trinity Broadcasting Network.

For information about special discounts for bulk purchases, please contact Trilogy Christian Publishing.

Manufactured in the United States of America

10 9 8 7 6 5 4 3 2 1

Library of Congress Cataloging-in-Publication Data is available.

ISBN 978-1-68556-977-8

ISBN 978-1-68556-978-5 (ebook)

DEDICATION

Robertice Hobbs "Dear"

Who showed me effective, efficient living long before I knew what I was seeing.

Anyone who knew her has a Dear story for every element in the 2 Peter formula.

ELEMENTS:

INTRODUCTION

Effective - accomplishing a purpose, producing the desired result

Efficient - producing the desired result without waste

Synonyms - productive, capable

Antonyms - fruitless, useless, wasteful, unproductive

One of my favorite pieces of jewelry is a simple charm bracelet given to me by some of my staff at Home National Bank (HNB). The charm and the people are what make it special. Engraved on the charm is this little emblem: E^2.

During my tenure in the HNB credit department, E^2 became our mantra. With every task, we asked these questions: "Is this effective and efficient? Are our processes accomplishing the desired results in the best possible manner?" Often in the professional world, this question asks whether we are striking the right balance between cost and results or we are properly balancing risk and return.

One day while reading 2 Peter, I discovered a formula for living effective, efficient lives! Formulas appeal to the credit analyst in me!

> *His divine power has given us everything we need for life and godliness through our knowledge of him who called us by his own glory and goodness. Through these he has*

7

given us his very great and precious promises, so that through them you may participate in the divine nature and escape the corruption in the world caused by evil desires.

For this very reason, make every effort to add to your faith goodness; and to goodness, knowledge; and to knowledge, self-control; and to self-control, perseverance; and to perseverance, godliness; and to godliness, brotherly kindness; and to brotherly kindness, love. For if you possess these qualities in increasing measure, they will keep you from being ineffective and unproductive in your knowledge of our Lord Jesus Christ.

2 Peter 1:3-8 NIV

Did you catch the formula? Faith + Goodness + Knowledge + Self-control + Perseverance + Godliness + Kindness + Love = Effective & Efficient Living!

In a drawer in my desk, I keep a few cards and notes from former bosses and employees expressing appreciation for a job well done, which I equate to effective, efficient work. Occasionally, I read them for encouragement when a task or situation frustrates me and remember all that was necessary to achieve whatever I was working on at that time.

My heart longs to be willing to do all that is necessary to hear Jesus express that my life has been a "job well done." I want my entire life, not just my professional life, to be E^2. This formula provides insight into how to accomplish that, and my heart tells me the formula is applicable to all areas of life.

In analysis, it is important to understand each element in a formula to accurately interpret the result. In measuring the effectiveness and efficiency of a process, each step must be considered. The chapters that follow analyze the 2 Peter formula by studying each element.

Before we look at the elements, we must have a clear picture of the desired result or purpose. That's a good place to start our analysis. What is the desired result of his divine power, glory, and goodness in our lives?

We find a strong clue in our key scripture: "...*So that* through them you may *participate in the divine nature* and *escape the corruption* in the world caused by evil desires" (2 Peter 1:4) (emphasis mine).

FAITH:
IS IT POSSIBLE?

Faith + Goodness + Knowledge + Self-Control + Perseverance + Godliness + Kindness + Love = Effective & Efficient Living!

Am I crazy to believe that it is possible to avoid quarrelling, outbursts of anger, selfish ambition, arrogance, greed, and other corrupt behaviors? In my professional world, these attitudes are frequently touted as ways to get things done, keep people in line, and protect your interests.

Is it possible to live a life filled with excellent and praiseworthy work, honest words, honorable plans, right decisions, pure motives, lovely thoughts, and admirable actions?

Before we start breaking down the formula, let's make sure we're on the same page. Participating in the divine

11

and avoiding the corrupt is not about avoiding people and things we have judged to be corrupt, nor is it about only hanging out with people and things we deemed to be divine. Nope, not at all. E² living is a life fully engaged with everyone and every responsibility God has placed in our life. The participation and the avoidance are about our hearts and our actions. As for me, this raises the question of whether this is possible to another level of concern!

When I was little, my mother was the youth leader at our church, which meant I attended youth rallies and parties long before I was a teenager. Shortly after my dad became a Christian, our family attended a youth rally at a church in a neighboring town. The special music guests that night were a group led by a man who worked for my dad at a plant years before. Dad had been a plant foreman with a reputation for making life difficult for the Bible school students that worked for him. The students had even referred to him as a Bible character: Balaam's "donkey".

When we walked into the youth rally, it was the first time this man had seen Dad since those days. He literally fell to his knees in shock when my dad walked into the church. Based on his experience, he must have thought it impossible, or at best highly unlikely, that he would ever see my dad at a church youth rally. But then, he didn't know about my mother's faith and how she knelt each night to pray for her husband's salvation. And he didn't know the faith and perseverance of our pastor, Walter Helms, who prayed, visited, and loved my dad.

Is it possible? The answer lies in the first component of our formula, faith! It is more than interesting that the first component is not self-control, knowledge, or perseverance. The first component has nothing to do with effort and everything to do with confidence. "Now faith is confidence in what we hope for and assurance about what we do not see" (Hebrews 11:1 NIV).

To complete any assignment effectively and efficiently, we must first understand the purpose and then believe it is possible. This principle is true in our homes, our churches, and our offices. The moment we lose confidence in a person, a company, or a process, we become ineffective. We may complete tasks, but we do not fully achieve the desired result.

So, how do we find this assurance of things we cannot yet see? I suggest that understanding our source is what gives us faith that a desired result is possible.

In credit analysis, second to understanding the purpose of a loan request is understanding the source of repayment. You can't have confidence that a loan will be repaid if you cannot accurately identify the source of repayment. Where will the borrower get the cash to repay the loan? Has it been sufficient in the past? Is it likely to continue?

So, what is our source for an E^2 life? Has it been sufficient in the past? Is it likely to continue?

> *His divine power has given us everything we need for life and godliness through our knowledge of him who called us by his own glory and goodness. Through these he has*

> *given us his very great and precious promises,*
> *so that through them you may participate in*
> *the divine nature and escape the corruption*
> *in the world caused by evil desires.*
>
> **2 Peter 1:3-4** NIV

Yes, his power has been sufficient in the past, and it is the only source we can know will continue to be sufficient in the future!

"It was by faith that Moses left the land of Egypt, not fearing the king's anger. He kept right on going because he kept his eyes on the one who is invisible" (Hebrews 11:27 NLT) I have often heard the term "blind faith". I propose that faith is not blind; it is keeping our eyes wide open and focused on our source.

I propose that faith is not blind; it is keeping our eyes wide open and focused on our source.

We may not see what lies ahead, but we see the source that is sufficient for whatever, whenever, wherever!

A debt service coverage ratio (DSCR) states the number of times an available source covers required debt payments. A DSCR of 2:1 simply means a borrower has $2 available for every $1 in required payments.

So, let's set up a coverage ratio for E^2 living:

Available Source = Faith in the One who has given us great and precious promises

Requirements of E^2 Living = Goodness, knowledge, self-control, perseverance, godliness, kindness, and love

Source / Requirements = A zillion, billion, million:1

It is sufficient! As one of my friends says, "Eyes on Jesus, Ronda! Eyes on Jesus!"

GOODNESS: BE GOOD!

Faith + Goodness + Knowledge + Self-control + Perseverance + Godliness + Kindness + Love = Effective & Efficient Living!

I've been told all my life to be good. When my mom told my brothers and me to be good at church, it meant to sit still, be quiet, and listen. When she told us to be good at school, it meant to obey the rules, listen to the teacher, and be nice to the other kids. When she told me to be good when I went on a date, it meant... Well, I'll let you fill in the blanks on that one!

Today, when I leave for work and my husband says to be good, it means to be quiet, listen ,and be nice to the other kids! Just kidding! It means to do the right things today.

So, what does it mean when Peter says to add goodness

to our faith? I think it means more than sit still, be quiet and play nice.

So far, we have discussed our need and hopefully kindled our desire to live E² lives. Lives seeking to achieve a purpose, which we have analyzed to be participating in the divine and avoiding the corrupt. We have calculated that faith in God's power is a sufficient source for the life we desire. With our eye on that source, let's begin our discussion of goodness.

"You are …God's very own possession. As a result, you can show others the goodness of God, for he called you out of the darkness into his wonderful light" (1 Peter 2:9 NLT). The parenthetical words are mine, not Peter's.

Logic requires that if we are going to show God's goodness to others, we need to understand his goodness. One definition offered by Webster for goodness is the best part of anything, the essence. As in, the essence of my job is the people. The essence of anything is that which defines it. Look at these verses with me, and let's see what we can learn about the goodness of God.

In the story of the Israelites, God and his people often refer to God's goodness, such as in Exodus 33. Moses asked God to show him his ways so that he might understand him more fully, to go with them and to show him His glorious presence. The Lord replied, "I will make all my goodness pass before you, …For I will show mercy to anyone I choose, and I will show compassion to anyone I choose" (Exodus 33:19 NLT). God chose to show mercy and compassion despite the sin of the people. He would go with them as Moses had asked.

Generations later, in Nehemiah 9, the people are recounting the history of their ancestors. Again and again, they rehearse the mercy and compassion shown by their God. In verse 35, they make this statement, "Even while they had their own kingdom, they did not serve you, though you showered your goodness on them" (NLT).

In Acts 14, Paul and Barnabas were sharing the Good News about the living God, and they said, "In the past he permitted all the nations to go their own ways, but he never left them without evidence of himself and his goodness". (Acts 14:16-17 NLT)

The Psalmist was confident he would see the Lord's goodness in the land of the living. (Psalm 27:13 NLT) He was confident goodness and mercy would follow him all the days of his life. (Psalm 23:6 NLT)

Over and over, in the account of God and his people, God's goodness is connected to his mercy and compassion. In the passage in Exodus, one of Moses' requests was that God show him His ways so that he might understand Him better. God responded by showing His mercy and compassion. This strongly suggests that the essence of the goodness of God is his mercy and compassion. Indeed, we would have no good news without his mercy and compassion!

Think of some of the good people in your life. Are mercy and compassion on the list of things that define them? I would venture to guess most of you would say yes. We know goodness when we experience it. So do the people you interact with every day.

We know goodness when we experience it. So do the people you interact with every day.

When I was a child, my Sunday school teacher would have us put our name in every time we read Israel in a verse. Try this one that way! It will motivate you to be good!

I will tell of the Lord's unfailing love.

I will praise the Lord for all he has done.

I will rejoice in his great goodness to Israel,

which he has granted according to his mercy and love.

Isaiah 63:7 NLT

KNOWLEDGE: INFORMED ACTIONS

Faith + Goodness + Knowledge + Self-Control + Perseverance + Godliness + Kindness + Love = Effective & Efficient Living!

In Chapter 2, we wrote a formula to measure the sufficiency of our source: faith in the One who has given great and precious promises, compared to the requirements of E^2 living. We determined that our source is abundantly adequate to meet the requirements.

I mentioned that in credit analysis it is critical to accurately identify the source of repayment. What I did not tell you is that it isn't as simple it might sound. The obvious answer is cash. In fact, cash is always the correct answer, but the analysis requires that you gain more knowledge about the source. How does the borrower generate cash? Do they sell a service or a product? If it is a product, do they make it or purchase it? How long does it take to sell the item and recover their cost? Do they sell on account? If so, how long does it take to collect on the account? The answers to these questions help to a gain a more complete understanding of the borrower's flow of cash or source.

If we are going to live E² lives, we need to go further than identifying our source. We need a more complete knowledge of our source. Just a few verses below our key passage, we find this advice from Peter on one way to increase our knowledge: "You must pay close attention to what they wrote, for their words are like a lamp shining in a dark place [corrupt]—until the Day dawns, and Christ the Morning Star shines in your hearts [divine]" (2 Peter 1:19 NLT). This reminds me of my dad frequently saying, "You've got to pay attention!"

In Paul's second letter to Timothy, he encourages Timothy to be a good (E²) worker. "All Scripture is inspired by God and is useful to teach us what is true and to make us realize what is wrong in our lives. It corrects us when we are wrong and teaches us to do what is right. God uses it to prepare and equip his people to do every good work" (2 Timothy 3:16-17 NLT). Paul's letters to Timothy are an excellent reminder of the things we seek to participate in and to avoid.

The reason we must pay close attention to His word is, as the Psalmist wrote, it is the light that shines on our path, showing us what is divine and what is corrupt. Without knowledge of His word, we don't know what to participate in and what to avoid. Knowledge of his word equips us to live E^2 lives!

Another element of analyzing a loan request is to evaluate management. An important question is whether they have the knowledge or know-how, as my dad would say, to achieve the desired result. This is best measured by actions and decisions previously made.

The entire premise of our E^2 formula begins with our knowledge of him and ends with our effectiveness in living in our knowledge of him. Our level of knowledge is demonstrated in our actions, which we begin looking at in Chapter 4.

We must be careful to remember that the reason we add knowledge is to inform our actions. Just as goodness is not possible without faith, knowledge is not productive without goodness.

> *Just as goodness is not possible without faith, knowledge is not productive without goodness.*

The end of our key passage reads this way, "The more you grow like this, the more productive and useful you will be in your knowledge of our Lord Jesus Christ" (2

Peter 2:18 NLT).

> *A few favorite Proverbs about knowledge:*
>
> *Intelligent people are always ready to learn.*
>
> *Their ears are open for knowledge.*
>
> **Proverbs 18:15** NLT

> *If you stop listening to instruction, my child,*
>
> *you will turn your back on knowledge.*
>
> **Proverbs 19:27** NLT

> *Fear of the LORD is the foundation of wisdom.*
>
> *Knowledge of the Holy One results in good judgment.*
>
> **Proverbs 9:10** NLT

> *The wise are mightier than the strong,*
>
> *and those with knowledge grow stronger and stronger.*
>
> **Proverbs 24:5** NLT

SELF-CONTROL: KILLER TOYS

Faith + Goodness + Knowledge + Self-Control + Perseverance + Godliness + Kindness + love = Effective & Efficient Living!

The joke among bankers in western Kansas when I was learning credit analysis was that you could always tell when it had been a good year for farmers by the number of new pickup trucks at the donut shop. When I attended Agricultural lending school, the instructor called these "killer toys." Killer toys were all the things, including new pickups, that farmers tended to believe they "needed" or deserved when production and prices were good. His theory was that the farmer with the fewest toys was the one who had the discipline to succeed in the years when production and/or prices were not so good. That principle was a good one to learn early in my career. It is one of the first things I analyze when looking at a new request.

What have they done with their cash in the past? Has their success resulted in growth in net worth (Net Worth = Assets – Liabilities, or as one of my favorite mentors would say, stuff minus bills.)? Over the years, I have seen the principle proven over and over again as the borrowers who lack the discipline to resist killer toys are the ones who end up on the bank's "problem list," and this is not an affliction unique to farmers.

If we are honest, we all have killer toys. Things, habits, or attitudes that pull us off track and interfere with our growth.

When I read Romans 8:3 (NLT), it is abundantly clear that our inability to control ourselves is nothing new. In fact, it is the very reason Christ came.

> *The law of Moses was unable to save us because of the weakness of our sinful nature. So, God did what the law could not do. He sent his own Son in a body like the bodies we sinners have. And in that body God declared an end to sin's control over us by giving his Son as a sacrifice for our sins.*
>
> **Romans 8:3** NLT

Because we could not control ourselves, Christ came to make it possible for us to live E² lives. That is a good God! That is knowledge that gives us hope and informs our actions.

In Galatians 5, Paul speaks to the Galatians about their freedom from the Law. He says that if they are trying to make themselves right or find favor with God by keeping the Law, they have forgotten the message of grace. This sounds like the same thing Peter said in our primary text about those who fail to grow according to the 2 Peter formula. They are shortsighted and have forgotten they have been cleansed from their sin. (2 Peter 1:9). So, one key to self-control is keeping our eye on our source! That sounds familiar.

"Let the Holy Spirit guide your lives. Then you won't be doing what your sinful nature craves" (Galatians 5:16 NLT). In the context of this book, we might say that the sinful nature wants to participate in the corrupt. Paul talks about the fighting within us, fighting to avoid the corrupt or working to achieve the divine. Neither can be done absent the guidance of the Holy Spirit.

The good news is that not only did he come to end sin's control, but also left his Spirit to produce results in us, including self-control (Galatians 5:23).

Self-control alone will not make us right or win us favor with God. Knowing His goodness, mercy, and compassion, we place our confidence in Him, and He provides His Spirit to assist us in our pursuit of E^2 lives. Lives that are not shortsighted or controlled by the corrupt but are instead productive, useful lives that reflect His goodness.

Lives that are not shortsighted or controlled by the corrupt, but are instead productive, useful lives that reflect His goodness

On those days when the "killer toys" are pulling our hearts and minds off track, let's not give in to being shortsighted. When you find angry words or clever lies on the tip of your tongue, remember the message of grace. Let's make good use of our knowledge of him and replace anger with mercy, selfish ambition with compassion, greed with generosity, arrogance with humility... I'll let you finish the list; you know your killer toys better than me.

I challenge you to do a little self-analysis. Are you making good use of your source, of His grace, His Spirit, and His Word? Are you growing in your desire to live a useful life? Can it be seen in your actions?

> *Since we are living by the Spirit, let us follow the Spirit's leading in every part of our lives.*
> **Galatians 5:25** NLT

PERSEVERANCE: NEVER GIVE UP!

Faith + Goodness + Knowledge + Self-Control + Perseverance + Godliness + Kindness + love = Effective & Efficient Living!

We ended Chapter 4 with this question: "Are you making good use of your source?" This next component definitely requires focus on our source! Just reading the definitions of some of the words used in various translations for this component makes me tired.

- Perseverance: steady persistence in a course of action, a purpose, especially despite difficulties, obstacles, or discouragement.

- Patient: bearing provocation, annoyance, misfortune, delay, hardship, pain, etc., with fortitude and calm and without complaint or anger

- Endurance: the ability or strength to continue or

last, especially despite fatigue, stress, or other adverse conditions

When managing a problem loan, there are two choices, often referred to as exit and rehab strategies. The exit strategy is the plan that gets the problem out of the bank the fastest. The exit strategy follows the philosophy that the earlier you call it, the less you lose; however, an exit strategy almost always involves loss for both parties. When all parties are willing to hang in there and work through a defined action plan to reach a mutual purpose, there is the possibility that no one will lose. While it takes more time and effort, when it is possible, it is the most rewarding.

I think those two strategies are applicable to most problem situations. The choice to exit, walk away, and give up is often tempting, but deciding to work through difficulties is the most rewarding—exhausting, aggravating, at times painful, but rewarding.

> *We can rejoice, too, when we run into problems and trials, for we know that they help us develop endurance. And endurance develops strength of character, and character strengthens our confident hope of salvation. And this hope will not lead to disappointment. For we know how dearly God loves us, because he has given us the Holy Spirit to fill our hearts with his love."*
>
> **Romans 5:3-5** NLT

We rejoice because we know that our faith in God, our

source for perseverance, and all the other E² elements, will not disappoint us. We can choose a rehab strategy and know that despite obstacles, discouragement, annoyance, delay, pain, and stress, we will not lose!

> *Therefore, since we are surrounded by such a huge crowd of witnesses to the life of faith, let us strip off every weight that slows us down, especially the sin that so easily trips us up. And let us run with endurance the race God has set before us. We do this by keeping our eyes on Jesus, the champion who initiates and perfects our faith.*
>
> **Hebrews 12:1-2** NLT

In E² words, let us avoid (strip away) the corrupt and participate with endurance in the divine, keeping our eyes on the source of faith.

"Because of the joy awaiting him, he endured the cross, disregarding its shame. Now he is seated in the place of honor beside God's throne. Think of all the hostility he endured from sinful people; then you won't become weary and give up" (Hebrews 12:2-3 NLT). That is perseverance! That is a Savior who stayed focused on his purpose and endured! When we think of all that He has done, we cannot give up!

Growing up with my mother, "Shut up" and "Give up" were not in our vocabulary. She thought "Shut up" was rude, and she did not believe in giving up. Whatever the task, she would find fun and often animated ways to help us through any assignment. She once chased me around the house making the sound of a mighty rushing wind and setting "flames" on my head. I was memorizing Acts 2, and I never forgot it!

Years later, when I was a young adult, she taught me a lesson in perseverance. And I never forgot it! Our family was experiencing one of those trials that bring pain and discouragement. I was ready for her to give up. I could not handle seeing her in pain. But she reminded me of another verse she had helped me memorize, 1 Corinthians 13. Sitting at my dining room table, she said, "Love always hopes, always perseveres. Love never fails." Some women may be Proverbs 31 women; my mother is a 1 Corinthians 13 woman. She knows her source and uses it well, despite difficulties.

In Galatians, we are encouraged not to get tired of doing what is good because at just the right time we will reap blessing (Galatians 6:9 NLT). To me, this means not to give up on participating in the divine even when the divine seems out of sight!

Do not give up on participating in the divine even when the divine seems out of sight!

In Matthew, we have another promise that carries us through rough places. Jesus tells us to come to Him, all of us who are weary, and He will give us rest, rest for our souls (Matthew 11:28-29). Yet another gift from the one who has given us great and precious promises!

Whatever is weighing you down and making it difficult to even see the divine, do not settle for an "exit" strategy. Find rest (rehab for your soul), keep your eyes on Jesus, and you will find hope to persevere in all things!

GODLINESS: RULES & WISHES

Faith + Goodness + Knowledge + Self-Control + Perseverance + Godliness + Kindness + Love = Effective & Efficient Living!

The bookshelf in my office is full of books of rules: Employee Handbooks, Loan Policies, Compliance Manuals, and volumes of Government Regulations. Employee handbooks are there to outline the wishes of management for employee conduct. Loan policies are there to enforce the wishes of the board of directors for risk tolerance. Compliance manuals are used to interpret the wishes of those who wrote the volumes of regulations! I am not a rules-oriented person. I wish everyone would just do the right thing. Ironically, much of my career has placed me in the role of the rule enforcer.

My goal is always to help a client or employee

understand the purpose of the rule, rather than simply demand adherence to the rule. I know it does not always work out that way, but when it does, I have an employee who is sync with the purpose of our work and capable of exercising judgment in carrying out their work. In short, I have an E² employee.

The rules are important but understanding the wishes of the ones who wrote the rules is critical to following them.

This brings us to our next element: godliness. Godliness is defined as conforming to the rules and wishes of God.

Scripture is full of rules. The Old Testament contains rules for seemingly everything under the sun—how to prepare sacrifices, how priests should dress, what and what not to eat, and of course, the Ten Commandments. In our study, we are analyzing a list from the New Testament of things to participate in and things to avoid. No doubt, there is a need for rules, but it is critical that we understand the wishes of the one who wrote the rules.

Each time Jesus is asked for the most important rule, his answers consistently come down to two things: love the Lord your God and love your neighbor. In these responses, we find clues about the wishes of God. When we conform to his wishes, conformity to his rules is a natural result. If we love our neighbor, we will not lie, cheat, nor steal from him.

It seems we often get confused and think conforming to his rules is his wish for us.

It seems we often get confused and think conforming to his rules is his wish for us.

This is nothing new. In Isaiah 58, the prophet deals with a similar problem in the children of Israel (As you read this, remember to substitute your name for Israel):

> *They come to the Temple every day*
> *and seem delighted to learn all about me.*
> *They act like a righteous nation*
> *That would never abandon the laws of its God.*
> *They ask me to take action on their behalf,*
> *pretending they want to be near me.*
> *"We have fasted before you!" they say.*
> *"Why aren't you impressed?*
> *We have been very hard on ourselves,*
> *and you don't even notice it!"*

Isaiah 58:2-3 NLT

Don't we sound this way sometimes? "I've done everything right, God, and you don't even notice." It sounds a lot like an employee who thinks they merit a promotion or a raise because they showed up on time every day and didn't even use all their sick days! Here is the problem the Lord pointed out:

> *It's because you are fasting to please yourselves.*
>
> *Even while you fast,*
>
> *you keep oppressing your workers.*
>
> *What good is fasting*
>
> *when you keep on fighting and quarreling?*
>
> *This kind of fasting*
>
> *will never get you anywhere with me.*
>
> *You humble yourselves*
>
> *by going through the motions of penance,*
>
> *bowing your heads like reeds*
>
> *bending in the wind.*
>
> *Do you really think this will please the Lord?*
>
> *No, this is the kind of fasting I want:*
>
> *Free those who are wrongly imprisoned;*
>
> *lighten the burden of those who work for you.*
>
> *Let the oppressed go free*
>
> *and remove the chains that bind people.*
>
> *Share your food with the hungry,*
>
> *and give shelter to the homeless.*
>
> *Give clothes to those who need them,*
>
> *and do not hide from relatives who need your help.*
>
> *Then your salvation will come like the dawn,*
>
> *and your wounds will quickly heal.*

Your godliness will lead you forward,

and the glory of the Lord will protect you from behind.

Feed the hungry,

and help those in trouble.

Then your light will shine out from the darkness,

and the darkness around you will be as bright as noon."

Isaiah 58:3-8, 10 NLT

These verses draw a picture of what it means to love our neighbor. Lighten the load of others by offering assistance, support, and encouragement. Free the oppressed and remove the fears and addictions that bind people by showing them Jesus and offering forgiveness. Don't be afraid to get involved. Reflect the light! Help those in trouble, and do not hide from them, not even your relatives!

Living this way is how we help others to participate in the divine and avoid the corrupt. Your godliness (conformity to his wishes) will lead you forward and bring healing! Looking for direction in a situation? Act in conformity with his wishes.

I had an employee who worked for me for several years. The longer she worked with me, the more we sounded alike, wrote alike, and thought alike. It was not that she had memorized all the policies and regulations. It was that she understood the purpose of our work and knew my wishes. She knew I hate all caps and prefer complete sentences to bulleted lists. More importantly, she knew that behind every financial statement we analyzed was a person. Because we were in sync, she was my "go to" person. She was someone I trusted completely to do the right thing, rules or no rules.

An E² follower is a "go to" person. One who knows and conforms to the wishes of the Father. One who can be trusted to do the right thing.

When I was a young teenager, I learned about the hymns and the authors. Fanny Crosby was one of my favorites. I think her hymn, "Recuse the Perishing" captures a glimpse of the wishes of God.

Rescue the perishing,

care for the dying,

Snatch them in pity from sin and the grave;

Weep o'er the erring one, lift up the fallen,

Tell them of Jesus, the mighty to save.

Though they are slighting Him,

still He is waiting,

Waiting the penitent child to receive;

Plead with them earnestly, plead with them gently;

He will forgive if they only believe.

Down in the human heart,

crushed by the tempter,

Feelings lie buried that grace can restore;

Touched by a loving heart, wakened by kindness,

Chords that were broken will vibrate once more.

KINDNESS: DIVINE INSPIRATION

Faith + Goodness + Knowledge + Self-Control + Perseverance + Godliness + Kindness + love = Effective & Efficient Living!

My first banking job was a teller position at a bank located in downtown Dallas. The ladies I worked with at the mini bank on the corner of 4th and Akard were very kind. They taught me everything I needed to know, not just the teller stuff, but also how to be safe in the parking garage, where to get the best deals on shoes, and how not to wear them out walking on the concrete! They shared with me the things I needed to know about our regular customers, especially the gentleman who gave great tips! I always thought it kind of them to take turns waiting on him rather than fight over it. Our little team of four was very effective and efficient. We often won the awards for accuracy and customer service.

I later worked as a utility teller and moved around to different locations. That is when I began to see why our team was so often the top-rated group. Other groups were not as kind. They fought over lunch times and other silly things. They never helped each other find mistakes. As a result, both employee and customer experiences were less satisfying. I learned that some of our regulars at 4th and Akard walked extra blocks and waited in line just to come to our location.

Kindness definitely has an impact of the effectiveness and efficiency of a group. It inspires us to participate in the divine. On the other hand, the absence of kindness generally yields corrupt behaviors, such as, quarrelling, outburst of anger and selfish ambition.

The absence of kindness generally yields corrupt behaviors, such as, quarrelling, outburst of anger and selfish ambition.

I believe this is exactly what Scripture is teaching us in Ephesians 4. The entire chapter is about living in unity as children of the light. God wants us to know that to operate effectively as a family, his children need to be kind to one another.

Get rid of all bitterness, rage, anger, harsh words, and slander, as well as all types of evil behavior. Instead, be kind to each other, tenderhearted, forgiving one another, just as God through Christ has forgiven you.

Ephesians 4:31-32 NLT

In every translation I've read, there is an adjective in front of kindness in our formula: brotherly. For me this adjective adds depth to the component of kindness. I have three brothers, and there is nothing I would not do for them. The kindness called for here is more than stopping to help a stranger along the way. It's more than being nice and extending common courtesies to our co-workers. It's about showing genuine care to those with whom we share life. Why? Because it conforms to the wishes of the One who has given us great and precious promises. The One who is our sufficient source for living. According to our key verses in 2 Peter 1, to do less would be shortsighted, forgetting the kindness He has shown us.

In Chapter 6, I shared the hymn, "Rescue the Pershing." The last stanza of the hymn offered further insight into the role of kindness in our E^2 formula:

Down in the human heart,

crushed by the tempter,

Feelings lie buried that grace can restore;

Touched by a loving heart, wakened by kindness,

Chords that were broken will vibrate once more. (Fanny Crosby)

At the beginning of our analysis, I proposed the desired result of his divine power, glory, and goodness in our lives to be participation in the divine and avoidance of the corrupt. I propose we add to our purpose to help others to participate in the divine and avoid the corrupt. A couple favorite quotes from Mother Teresa and Mark Twain provide further insight into the importance of kindness:

"I prefer you to make mistakes in kindness than work miracles in unkindness" (Mother Teresa).

"Kindness is a language which the deaf can hear and the blind can read" (Mark Twain).

LOVE:
THE BOTTOM LINE

Faith + Goodness + Knowledge + Self-Control + Perseverance + Godliness + Kindness + Love = Effective & Efficient Living!

Any complete analysis ultimately comes down to a bottom line. In loan analysis, the bottom line always involves cash. Sufficient cash for a down payment, sufficient cash to start a business or sufficient cash to make the payments. Any way you slice it, the bottom line comes back to cash.

In our last component, I think we've found the bottom line of our analysis. E² lives cannot happen without love—accepting God's love, returning God's love, and sharing God's love. Any way you slice it, the bottom line comes back to love. This is the message of 1 Corinthians 13: "the greatest of these is love." If that is not sufficient evidence to support my analysis, let's look at Jesus' reply when asked for the "bottom line" in Mark, Chapter 12. Jesus replied,

> *The most important commandment is this: "Listen, O Israel! The Lord our God is the one and only LORD. And you must love the Lord your God with all your heart, all your soul, all your mind, and all your strength." The second is equally important: "Love your neighbor as yourself." No other commandment is greater than these.*

> **Mark 12:29-31** NLT

It all begins with our acceptance of his love for us: a love that makes it possible for us to participate in the divine and avoid the corrupt.

> *God showed how much he loved us by sending his one and only Son into the world so that we might have eternal life through him. This is real love—not that we loved God, but that he loved us and sent his Son as a sacrifice to take away our sins.*

> **1 John 4:9-10** NLT

God's love is a love that makes it possible for us to help others know the divine and avoid the corrupt.

> *Dear friends, since God loved us that much, we surely ought to love each other. No one has ever seen God. But if we love each other, God lives in us, and his love is brought to full expression in us.*

> **1 John 4:11-12** NLT

My brother sang a song when we were younger that said it this way: "I am loved, you are loved, I can risk loving you, for the one who knows me best, loves me most. That's the bottom line!"

Love is the best motivator. The days I love my job and the people with whom I work are by far the most effective and efficient, productive, and useful days.

When I first started learning to analyze financial statements, I was not aware of the practice of dropping the last three digits of the numbers in most printed reports. Recognizing this practice completely changed what I was seeing; $100,000 is completely different than $100. Love is the most powerful element of our formula. It is like adding zeros to a number; it completely changes the result!

> *Love is the most powerful element of our formula. It is like adding zeros to a number; it completely changes the result!*

This verse from Romans, sums up the bottom line:

> *Don't just pretend to love others. Really love them. Hate what is wrong. Hold tightly to what is good. Love each other with genuine*

affection, and take delight in honoring each other. Never be lazy but work hard and serve the Lord enthusiastically.

Romans 12:9-11 NLT

In E2 words, we must honestly love each other. Hate the corrupt. Hold tightly to the divine. Love each other with brotherly kindness. Never be useless and unproductive but work effectively and efficiently and serve the Lord enthusiastically.

"Enthusiastically," I love that "E" word. It makes me think of when my mom would tell my brother to do something with a twinkle in his eye. Maybe it's E^3? Living effectively and efficiently, with enthusiasm.

May you experience the love of Christ, though it is too great to understand fully. Then you will be made complete with all the fullness of life and power that comes from God.

Ephesians 3:19 NLT

CONCLUSION

Faith + Goodness + Knowledge + Self-Control + Perseverance + Godliness + Kindness + Love = Effective & Efficient Living!

> *His divine power has given us everything we need for life and godliness through our knowledge of him who called us by his own glory and goodness. Through these he has given us his very great and precious promises, so that through them you may participate in the divine nature and escape the corruption in the world caused by evil desires.*
>
> *For this very reason, make every effort to add to your faith goodness; and to goodness, knowledge; and to knowledge, self-control; and to self-control, perseverance; and to perseverance, godliness; and to godliness, brotherly kindness; and to brotherly kindness, love. For if you possess these qualities in*

> *increasing measure, they will keep you from being ineffective and unproductive in your knowledge of our Lord Jesus Christ.*
>
> **2 Peter 1:3-8** NIV

One of the more experienced lenders I worked with often referred to a rookie's analysis as an "elevator" analysis. By this he meant it covered all the necessary points with the proper words and ratios, but in the end, it drew no useful conclusions. Hoping to avoid that rookie trap, allow me to offer some conclusions I pray will be useful.

Christ desires that our lives produce useful results. Results that do not waste the great and precious gifts he has given. He wishes us to actively participate in the divine—good and right things—and avoid corrupt or evil things.

- Goodness is the essence of something or someone. When asked to show his goodness, God showed his mercy and compassion.

- Knowledge yields informed action. It is knowledge of His Word that helps us to know what to participate in and what to avoid.

- Self-Control is possible because of Christ. Because of our inability to control ourselves, Christ came to win control over sin and left his Spirit to produce this same victory in us.

- Perseverance is necessary. Never give up! When we keep our eyes on Jesus, the source of our faith, we can choose a rehab strategy over an exit strategy.

- Godliness is conforming to the wishes of God. Lighten the load of others. Reflect the light. Help those in trouble.

- Kindness inspires us and others to participate in the divine. The absence of kindness generally yields quarrelling, outbursts of anger and selfish ambition, all on the list of the corrupt.

- Love is the great motivator for all the above!

If you take anything from this analysis, I hope it will be that Christ has provided all that we need to live effective, useful lives. He has not only given us instructions on how to live; He has provided the motivation to live this way.

My least productive days have been when a boss has given an ultimatum, particularly one that came with no instruction; however, I have worked long, productive days for a boss who elicited high performance, not only with words but also with actions.

I respond best to a boss who understands what is required to complete an assignment: one who is willing to leave the corner office and work alongside me to achieve the desired result. This boss provides all the resources necessary to accomplish the task effectively and efficiently. That kind of boss demands my best effort.

While Christ has given us an ultimatum, He has also provided all the instructions we need. He Himself left His place in Heaven to not only walk where I would walk but also to give his life to make mine possible. He understands much better than I all that is required to complete any assignment. He left His Spirit to work alongside me to achieve the desired result. He provided the template for an E² life: one filled with faith, goodness, knowledge, self-control, perseverance, godliness, kindness, and love. That kind of Savior demands my best effort!

> *Now all glory to God, who is able, through his mighty power at work within us, to accomplish infinitely more than we might ask or think.*
>
> **Ephesians 3:20** NLT

ABOUT THE AUTHOR

"Here's the church, and here's the steeple; open it up, and here's all the people." Ronda describes herself as one of the people in that old children's poem: one who is lucky enough to have lived life in the shadow of the steeple.

She and her husband, Stephen, have been married for 38 years and have spent 25 of those years in Christian ministry.

Her banking career began with a bank teller position to help pay for college. Along the way, she found a passion for the numbers and for the stories of the people behind them. She has spent the last fifteen years serving as a senior member of bank management teams as a Chief Credit Officer. Even there, she finds that the lessons learned from parents, pastors, and Sunday School teachers are the ones that give the clearest direction.

Ronda has a bachelor's degree in Business and a Master of Banking. She currently resides in Edmond, Oklahoma.